The Words Unsaid

a collection of poems

Muskaan Bhagat

pencil

ISBN 978-93-5667-159-1
© Muskaan Bhagat 2022
Published in India 2022 by Pencil

A brand of
One Point Six Technologies Pvt. Ltd.
123, Building J2, Shram Seva Premises,
Wadala Truck Terminal, Wadala (E)
Mumbai 400037, Maharashtra, INDIA
E connect@thepencilapp.com
W www.thepencilapp.com

CONTENTS

Introduction

A collection of poems written as an expression of varied emotions felt by each one of us while strolling through the years of youth.

It feels like riding a roller coaster. At times we feel like we can move the world and at other times unreciprocated feelings make us feel like there's nothing good left in life. We want the life of our dreams and are motivated to work for it but at the same time we are driven by the urge to do all the crazy stuff that make no sense. We feel like we are alone but in reality we are connected by these amalgam of emotions with each one of us containing different proportion of its component.

These poems touch upon all these feelings which each one of us feel. The hope, the love, the hurt, the longing, the admiration, the confusion, the identity crisis, the chaos.

A Way of life - the vibe

1

"The world is a chaotic place and so is our mind. Yet to give ourselves a sense of control we create routines and regulations. What should we do and what should we not. Doing things a certain way and thinking in conventional ways is expected firstly from ourselves and then from everyone else. And when anyone dares to be different. They are labelled to be rebel or as far stretched as crazy."

1. A Way of Life

<u>A WAY OF LIFE</u>

Ignoring the noises of the worldly crowd

Listening to the music of my beating heart

Residing in this world for the sake of my world

Even if my world is a universe apart

Pretendence for acceptance is must for existence

Is taught to a kid learning to stand on tiny toes

Yet I chose to forget myself in love for self

Leaving behind the idea of friends & foes

Headed towards my world of dreams

Where fire is in harmony with snow

Lies in galaxy of peace and universe of compassion

Is all what my heart speaks & senses know

Mind is imprisoned by idea of success

Heart clutched in chains of definition of free

Neither loved and free nor cherished and understood

Now abandoned is what my soul seeks to be!

The Adjective - the vibe

2

"Sometimes it becomes difficult to define your feelings in words. No matter how accurately anybody says that word can describe a feeling but sometimes the feeling in your chest feels too big and pure for any kind of description. The only language in which it can be described is that of eyes. And the beauty of this language is that it can only be understood by the one to whom it is spoken to."

2. The adjective

<u>THE ADJECTIVE</u>

And when they inquired, "What is it that you feel?"
They expected me to answer in a word.
Just one word, What a shame!
How could I, ever, possibly squeeze everything I feel in
one word?
What a mockery it would have been!
Giving a word to my feelings and watching the world ruin
it's essence.
Just like they ruined "Love"
and now It's nothing more than moments of lust.
Or Just like they ruined "Heaven"
and now even the stairs to hell are said to end there.
Or Just like they ruined "Forever"
and now It is limited to minute periods of physical
togetherness.
Or Just like they ruined "Soul",
for now It belongs to everything they have ever touched.
So tell me how could I dishonour my feelings just like
that?
I would rather make it known to him
Through gestures and Smiles

Through eye contacts and heartbeats
But not in a language that the world understands.
For it loves to ravage,
Ravage whatever it finds beautiful!

Heartache - the vibe

3

" It's not always possible to explain what goes inside our head and how the heart suffers. That feeling of emptiness overpowers our sanity and all we can think of is pain. The pain we carry in our hearts and The pain that becomes a part of us. And what hurts even more is the reason causing this hurt (also the reason that can end this ache) would never even know about the suffering!"

3. Heartache

HEARTACHE

You know it hurts?

Not knowing what to do.
Being so passive.
And waiting for things to get better.
You know it hurts?
Waiting for you
Imagining the moment when I'll see you
Fantasising the conversation between us
That never gonna happen.
You know it hurts ?
Feeling as if there is a hole in chest
And surviving it's burning edges
That tries to shut it close
More like a physical pain than an abstract emotion.
You know it hurts?
Knowing it would never matter to you.
Realising the pain would last longer
Than I would ever be able to endure.
Most importantly,
You know it hurts?

The Words Unsaid

To never be able to accept
That how much it actually hurts!

Unexpressed - the vibe

4

"(How do you mourn the loss of a love you never spoke out loud

never felt with your own two hands?"

-Shelby Eileen, soft in the middle)

A quote so beautiful yet so heart-breaking. But the feeling that it talks about is even more complicated to feel. The feeling of being so much in love, The sorrow of being separated from that love and the hope of being united in love and the agony of being helpless in the moment- the person feels all of this at once. But we have to keep moving."

4. Unexpressed

<u>UNEXPRESSED</u>

Unspoken love like unanswered prayer

Keeps echoing in the perceived heavens

Until it manifests or completely shatters your faith

You never loudly grieve for that lost love

For you do not complaint about the suffering

when you keep hidden the parts of you scathed

So you keep it in, shut tightly in all the empty spaces you can find

Until it outgrows your being and explodes

Causing the damage so quietly and seamlessly yet so profound.

As it flow from the slits of your tightly closed eyes

And recently formed cracks in your heart

You let that lava burn everything within and around.

You mourn by craving stolen glances

And let your soul suffer by avoiding eye contacts.

With every person they smile with, you repent by making yourself jealous

You would yearn for them to hold you and love you back

But then you'll realise

How much you really have to break your heart to save it
from being broken by someone else.

Hope - the vibe

5

"Sometimes things are so obvious and clear before our eyes, but the hope within our hearts do not cease to read between the lines. It wants things to change , change to become the way it always wanted them to be.

But they don't and an overly hopeful heart becomes a problem in its own."

5. Hope

<u>HOPE</u>

Hope is a cruel, cruel thing

It sees the blooming flower

In a day old bud

It loves its petals even before they exist

And cherish its fragrance before it spreads.

When they say it makes us live

They mean it makes us live in daydream

In illusion of what could have had been

In nostalgia of what never happened.

And at the end it stabs us

At parts we left bare for it

To touch and heal.

It betrays us in most heart breaking ways

As it never prepares us for what happens after that bud
dies

Even before those petals could ever know sunshine.

It just leaves

And leaves so innocently

As if it never committed any crime

Leaving us pondering

On what is causing this pain when everything is just the same.

Leaving us gasping

At extent of empty space it leaves in our hearts.

To and fro - the vibe

6

"Mixed signals are already irritating enough to deal with but when they come from the person you have truckloads of feelings for , it makes you loose your sleep.

You want it to be a yes so bad but in order to not look like a fool you overthink their every action to be a no.

You know in your heart that those eye contacts mean something but your mind speaks loud and clear when it says, " they would have if they wanted it to be."

In these moments of chaos , all you want is clarity which can only come from someone else and you can do nothing but wait."

6. To and Fro

<u>TO AND FRO</u>

I hesitantly race my eyes up to yours

More often the not find them glancing at mine

I am not here for fun and games

Either make it known in the right way

Or do not let them eyes to intertwine.

Look at me and say out loud

What is it you feel about me ?

Dare not think you can juggle me like that

For I won't stick around waiting forever

If one of your side muse is all you want me to be.

I don't fear rejections or heartbreaks

If you have to break my heart, just break it right away

I can't take second guessing and mix signals no more

What I am afraid of is being cheated and played

So I beg you not to keep me leading on a blind ended way.

My mind plays our differences on loop

but emotions keep flowing from my eyes.

In darkness of my thoughts, I want your love to be the
light.

For us to be together, you would have to rebel

I am ready to risky it all

But are you, too, willing to fight?

I ran away and then ran back to these feelings so many
times

I can't do it anymore for my legs hurt now

I don't know if I am taking a break or giving up on you

I have already taken too long to accept what I had known
all along

I know I have to move on ,I am just figuring out, how?

Deja vu - the vibe

7

"Moving in cycles and being unable to break away.

We feel like we are pulling away from that person but it's only matter of sometime that we tend to fall back in the same pattern.

You know nothing will come out of it so you try to take yourself away but your feelings overpowers you and one sign from them make you down spiral into falling for them again.

And the cycles continues."

7. Deja vu

<u>DEJA VU</u>

And there I stood again.

Having perhaps the Deja vu.

But haven't it happened before?

I don't know and I am too afraid to recall.

Did I Love you once before?

I think I did.

This time it was definitely much more.

This time it was mixed with happiness and hope.

Did you make me feel wanted once before?

May be you did.

May be you did not.

But I perceived so.

Once before too I had felt these butterflies in my stomach
go crazy over you.

Did you once lock your eyes with mine before?

Like a dream in deep sleep,

I only can recall haziness all around.

I only remembered your eyes I stared into.

Don't ask me more about it.

For I barely have my senses with have my eyes on yours.

Did you me left me feeling worthless once before?

Yes I remember that precisely.

That pain I felt, the tears I shed.

The emptiness in my chest I felt.

It hardly lets me forget its every detail.

And here I stand yet again.

Thinking about you.

Having perhaps the Deja vu.

Fragrance of Sorrow - the vibe

8

"Sadness- a feeling of which nobody is oblivious of. We all have experienced it and sometime long enough to make it a part of our lives and some situations bring out this feeling without being inherently sorrowful.

Like a rainy night or a piece of music.

Sometimes it's just a thought about a human who may have done nothing wrong to say but whenever you think of them all you can feel is a feeling of deep melancholy."

8. Fragrance of Sorrow

<u>FRAGRANCE OF SORROW</u>

If melancholy was fragrant

What do you think it would smell like?

Would it smell like a rainy night?

Cradling my insecurities, humming lullabies to my smile

Thick with the scent of dark desires and putting to sleep
my inner light

Or would it smell like withering flowers?

Unappealing to eyes, carrying rejection to their core

In love with the Sun and praying for showers

Or would it smell like old, worn out pages?

Read and scribbled and scratched and torn

Stripped of life, and not glanced at from ages.

Or may be it would smell just like you

Dysphoric gust of fragrance that clouds my mind

It smells exactly like your apathy mixed with my rue!

The Deal - the vibe

9

"Lovers would make the worst negotiators. For they are willing to give their everything to the person for them to just be there and to see them smile.

Many a times they give away so much, if not everything, for nothing. Nothing else makes sense other than offering their loyalty, time, heart, soul and life to the person who gave them a chance to experience this pure feeling."

9. The Deal

<u>THE DEAL</u>

Let me stay

You have the shelter and I have no where to go

I can stand the Sun

I can bear the Rain

I have loved the Moon

I have danced on the Waves

I am gentle enough to walk on thin ice

I am capable enough to tame the Storms

But today I want something less

Less than what I have had

Today I just want to feel the warmth

And comfort

And kindness

And love

So let me in and give me your time

Few days

Or some hours

Or just seconds.

I will be happy to have even a moment

For in that moment I will give you my eternity

But I know even my eternity will fall short

So why don't you trade all your moments

for all of my eternities?

I know I will be at loss

But it's okay as it would be worth

To lose all my eternities for all those moments of 'US'.

Love Personified - the vibe

10

"When in love, nobody compares to the person that stirred those feelings in us. Everything about them causes our heart to race and breath to stop. We are in so much awe and the admiration for them ,more often than not, crosses the humanly limit.And the desire to have them as close to the skin as anything can get seems powerful enough to burn anything that comes in way.That person for us is Love."

10. Love Personified

<u>LOVE PERSONIFIED</u>

On a serious note

Have someone ever told you how gorgeous you are?

'coz you are such a beauty

I look at you like a kid witnessing firework

Wanting to reach for it , astonished and amazed

That I forget how to breathe ,let alone talk

After taking even a glance at your face.

I cannot help

But to love your eyes

Those pretty pretty jars of chocolate

So dark and so calm

So magnetic yet so delicate

With all the strength I have

I try to resist myself to stare at them

Every second, all day long

As tempting and addicting they are

Needless to say, every single time I fail.

I want to capture your face

The Words Unsaid

In all different emotions

With these tiny eyes of mine

I want you to sit close to me

Smiling gently and not saying a word

Letting me appreciate the work of art you are

Letting me absorb your every bit, your every part.

I want to say your name over and over

With love and with desire

With need and with desperation

In situations where it's forbidden

At times when it's unexpected

And I yearn to hear my name

Coming out of your mouth

Like it's the only thing you could remember

Like it is the chant keeping you alive

I hope you won't mind

When I'll tell you I love you with all my soul

And you are what I desire.

And would you mind if I confessed

I crave to put my fingertips lovingly on your lips

Tracing with them, the curve of your smile.

Or I would love to press my lips gently

On the closed lids of your eyes.

Or I fancy to be embraced so tightly in your arms with my
face buried in your chest

That I forget this world, my existence and this life.

Detached - the vibe

11

"There are times when we feel everything we expose ourselves to will ultimately hurt us. We have been wounded so much for so long by the things and people we surround ourselves with that we feel comfort in isolation, knowing nobody can reach us there.

Sometimes it more than just that. Sometimes we can't just help ourselves to bring ourselves to socialise. It's more of a mental struggle. But in such dark times, we must not feel ashamed to ask for help.

No matter what our noisy mind says we must remember even if we can't turn the lights on for ourselves, there are people in our lives who would be willing to draw the curtains and let the sunlight come in.

11. Detached

<u>DETACHED</u>

I love the walls high, curtains drawn

Doors closed and lights dimmed

I feel better alone, in the dark

Hidden in shadows, invisible and obscured.

For I know it's hard!

It's painfully hard to fill the voids

In our lives, In our hearts

In our souls, In our eyes.

Voids left by the ones we once we loved.

But I fear I shall reap what I have sown

And from love & attachment blooms pain

So trust me when I say, "I'm better off alone!"

The Dilemma - the vibe

12

"We are such greedy people.

We want everything. We want to be cuddled like a baby. We also want to be the one to change the narrative.

We want flowers with forehead kisses. We also want to be independent ,strong individuals that needs no one.

We want it all for ourselves.

It's the never ending dilemma. It's never ending fight of ourselves with ourselves."

12. Dilemma

THE DILEMMA

Some of these days, the voices in my head talk

And as a listener I believe they have some serious issue

Having one conversation over and over again

One voice talked about the love and romance

Of that young girl that has just found her world

In the scent of the roses and touch of the wind

In warmth of her lover's presence and safety of his strong arms

The love starved girl in me craved to lunge into that forbidden sea of its words

Then there is something in me that says, "Love only belongs to fictions and fairytales."

Then there is another voice that presented a strong vision.

The vision of freedom and independence

No strings attached expressed and no feelings expressed

Unbecoming the the person I show and becoming the person I hide

Just me in my world, dying for no one living for no cause

Living like a nomad beyond what's happy and sad

Being in this body and yet so far.

I sit there silently listening to them, not participating

Reassuring myself it doesn't concern me

But knowing one day I'd have to favour one

Not just to choose but to become one.

The Space Where I Exist - the vibe

13

"So many questions unanswered. So many mysteries unresolved. How everything happens? Why everything happens? Is everything preplanned? Is everything is just a organised mess?We all want answers but may be it's better to be in bliss of ignorance."

13. The Space Where I Exist

<u>THE SPACE WHERE I EXIST</u>

A never changing folktale

Or story with a plot twist

Which of two I'm a part of?

I want to know the space where I exist

Am I the only one abandoned here?

Or you too feel this cold, all consuming mist?

Where I can not judge even a step ahead

Is it our destiny, they say, we predict?

We are nothing but part of a scripted play

Whatever happens is meant to be, they insist

Do we never really get to choose?

Is there nothing we willingly attract or resist?

Although my eyes find everything unadorned

But my reluctance to accept it incessantly persist

As truths are hidden in complexities of simplicity

Am I even supposed to know the place where I exist?

The Sanctuary - the vibe

14

" We are restless roaming beings in search of peace. We want a stable life with a sense of safety. While this might not be possible in every moment of our life but we strive to find ourselves home where we can rest our tired souls and over worked minds.

Everyone of us built their own such homes in unique calming places and find abode of lifetime."

14. The Sanctuary

<u>THE SANCTUARY</u>

We race and We chase

We desire and We achieve

But never so much to keep us satisfied.

We discover And We accept

We love and We preach

But never enough to keep our insecurities quiet.

We are same, We are similar

We are varied, We are different

All pacing in random directions with a sole intention.

Everyone doing everything they can

Only to find a hiding place.

A place to put our baggage down

When this world becomes too much

Or When our responsibilities overwhelm us.

A hiding place to remind us of our authentic being

When our minds become too loud

And our hearts become too heavy.

And the beauty lies in the fact that

This place is not a fixed destination.

It can be in anyone, anything, anywhere

Wherever our soul feels home

Wherever our subconscious finds peace.

May be you find it in the boundaries of your house

May be they find in someone's voice and hugs

May be I find it in my solitude and writing unsaid words.

Everything we do is just trying and testing

To be there and make it our forever homes.

Not that life stops being sadist after that

The battles continue and so do the celebrations

But we find a sense of harmony within us

Knowing we have somewhere to return.

Maze of Hearts - the vibe

15

"Each one of us deserves to be loved the right way. The honest, unapologetic, passionate kind of love.But when unable to receive that we atleast deserve the clarity on where we stand.What can hurt more than rejection is not knowing where do we stand in someone's life.We deserve to be accepted with whole heart or set free from the connection."

15. Maze of hearts

<u>MAZE OF HEARTS</u>

I am more than willing to live in this place

Called hope

I am willing to make to it my home

Waiting for the happily ever after

But would you mind turning few of its lights on?

Just enough for me to see few steps ahead

As from where I am at this moment

It seems like sea of endless nights

And I am paralysed by the fear

The fear of this creeping darkness

The fear of never finding my way out

The fear of being left with just sadness and regrets

The regret of "what ifs" and "could have beens"

And of all the daydreams and fantasies

That might have turned into real moments and things

And all the wait that would have been worth

Only if I knew how much to wait.

But this place where I am

Does not allow me to speak out loud and ask you for it

Because another fear cripples and muffles my voice

That my plea will be denied

Or even worse I fear you might never respond

Making me feel as if this was mere an illusion

All in my head

All just a dream.

And I fear I'll have to find windows to breaks

Falling and hurting

shouting and sobbing

In this maze, looking for an escape.

Silent Sobs - the vibe

16

"No one understands, including us, how and when did we give so much power over us to someone who could , intentionally or unintentionally, break our heart so badly.We pray for the heavy, crushing feelings to leave our heart but as they say it happens over time.Time which may be counted in weeks or months by people but lived as number of tears and amount of heartache by the one hurting. Each moment passing with the belief that this ,too, shall pass!"

16. Silent Sobs

<u>SILENT SOBS</u>

I lie awake on my bed

Night after another

Letting my feelings burn a hole inside my chest

Gradually and effortlessly.

Screams and sobs waiting to escape

As spontaneously as tears from my eyes

But I purse my lips

I clench my teeth

I bite my tongue

I choke on my tears

Keeping proofs of my defeat locked in my throat.

I do not question

I do not complaint

Gracefully I let pain sweep all over me

And I let myself immerse deep into ocean of agony.

This is not my fate

But this is the choice I had made

To stay here

To let myself suffocate.

For dying seemed easier

Than to let myself feel again

But what's scarier is this thought

That I would have to stay here forever

Not allowing myself to live

And not knowing how to completely surrender myself to
death.

Musical Dreams - the vibe

17

*"Music heals and music brings out the deep buried emotions.
Sometimes you listen, sometimes you hum along and sometimes you
sing your heart out.*

*But it becomes a little too much to take when your heart desire to
hear the melodies coming out of their mouth just for you.*

Isn't it the most romantic gesture?

Singing for your love and meaning everything you sing.

I don't want a lot but I want this."

17. Musical Dreams

<u>MUSICAL DREAMS</u>

I think of the moments bygone

Pretending to command their impact begone

In hope of seeking answers to my doubts

In nights full of silences

I ask your shadows to sing me a song

Little melodies.

Murmur of verses.

Or just a monologue,

Straight outta heart.

May be mess up some lyrics

Just so we can have a good laugh.

Perhaps you can scream some lines at top of your lungs,

For the world to listen.

And can simply whisper some of them close to my ears,

For just me to hear.

Just sing me a song

This would be the least you can do.

This would be the most you can do.

Please sing me a song

Is it too big a thing to ask?

52

Muse - the vibe

18

"How beautiful it is to be able to express yourself and the beauty becomes manifolds when you make art out of it. But we need to talk about the time when that feelings wane or worse, that become opposite to the initial feeling. Love becomes hate and peace becomes hurt. Do the artist feel the initial emotion while revisiting the work or the current emotions overpowers to find the flaws in the piece?"

18. Muse

<u>MUSE</u>

I read somewhere:

"To make someone a part of your art is the greatest
expression of love."

And I couldn't have agreed more!

What could be better then being able to find oneself in
someone's words?

See one's reflection in someone's colours?

Hear love for oneself in someone's voice?

I ,too, could do that for you.

Make you a part of my art.

I could write each day everyday for you

To keep you forever with me in my poems

Preserved for eternity ,written in my ink.

But that's what I fear too

Having you forever in my words

In my diary.

Even when I wouldn't want you to be there anymore.

So before I do this for you

Make me feel you are worthy enough

For me to be stuck with you forever.

Even when I wouldn't want to be stuck with you.

55

Perception - the vibe

19

"If somebody would ask us to list our flaws, we would write everything we can possibly think of but if asked to say even a few of our qualities we would hardly have anything to say.

Self love is something we all preach but it is also something we all lack.

Imagine how beautiful that feeling would be to know someone loves us unconditionally, indefinitely.

So Why not be that person for ourselves?"

19. Perception

<u>PERCEPTION</u>

Why is that we are able to see good in others so easily?

Small details and all so beautiful

Nothing flawed

Nothing ugly

Nothing almost perfect

Just an individual perfectly beautiful

But when it comes to ourselves

Why do we become so harsh?

So emotionless ?

So unempathetic?

And all we can see are our flaws

In every bit, in every part

Feelings apologetic for the scars which defines our existence

Don't we, ourselves, need the compassion we shower on others

Why can't we be the first receiver of the love we give out in the universe?

Just why?